EYEWITNESS ● READERS

Level 4
GRADES 2-4

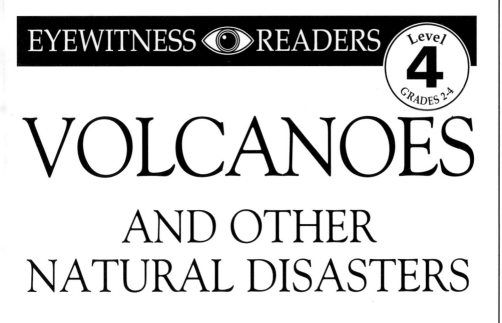

VOLCANOES

AND OTHER NATURAL DISASTERS

Written by Harriet Griffey

D0097399

DK PUBLISHING, INC.

Floodwater
Torrential rain can cause river-banks to burst.

Planet power!

Volcanoes, earthquakes, tidal waves, hurricanes, flash floods, and forest fires – nature running wild is both spectacular and terrifying.

Despite all our modern resources, natural disasters still devastate lives.

Long Island, NY
(Hurricane, 1938)
Fierce storm winds whipped up huge waves and ravaged the eastern coast of the United States.
See pages 32–37.

Lisbon, Portugal
(Earthquake, 1755)
Earth tremors and fires devastated Portugal's capital.
See pages 14–17.

PACIFIC
OCEAN

NORTH
AMERICA

EUROPE

ATLANTIC
OCEAN

AFRICA

SOUTH
AMERICA

San Francisco, CA
(Earthquake, 1906)
The city was shaken to the ground and then consumed by fire.
See pages 26–31.

Yungay, Peru
(Avalanche, 1970)
In the mountains of Peru, an avalanche of ice and rock buried the people of Yungay alive.
See pages 38–41.

Martinique, Caribbean
(Volcano, 1902)
The terrible eruption of Mount Pelée destroyed the port of St. Pierre.
See pages 22–25.

A Note to Parents

Eyewitness Readers is a compelling new program for beginning readers, designed in conjunction with leading literacy experts, including Dr. Linda Gambrell, President of the National Reading Conference and past board member of the International Reading Association.

Eyewitness has become the most trusted name in illustrated books, and this new series combines the highly visual *Eyewitness* approach with engaging, easy-to-read stories. Each *Eyewitness Reader* is guaranteed to capture a child's interest while developing his or her reading skills, general knowledge, and love of reading.

The four levels of *Eyewitness Readers* are aimed at different reading abilities, enabling you to choose the books that are exactly right for your children:

Level 1, for **Preschool to Grade 1**
Level 2, for **Grades 1 to 3**
Level 3, for **Grades 2 and 3**
Level 4, for **Grades 2 to 4**

The "normal" age at which a child begins to read can be anywhere from three to eight years old, so these levels are intended only as a general guideline.

No matter which level you select, you can be sure that you are helping your child learn to read, then read to learn!

A DK PUBLISHING BOOK
www.dk.com

Editors Rachel Wardley,
Steve Setford, and Lara Tankel
Designer Andrew Burgess
Senior Editor Linda Esposito
US Editor Regina Kahney
Deputy Managing Art Editor
Jane Horne
Production Kate Oliver
Picture Researcher Angela Anderson
Illustrator Peter Dennis

Reading Consultant
Linda B. Gambrell, Ph.D.

First American Edition, 1998
6 8 10 9 7
Published in the United States by
DK Publishing, Inc.
95 Madison Avenue, New York, New York 10016

Griffey, Harriet.
  Volcanoes and other natural disasters / written by Harriet Griffey.
    p. cm. — (Eyewitness readers. Level 4)
  Summary: Describes natural disasters which have occurred in various
places throughout the world including the eruption of Vesuvius in 79 A.D.,
the Yellow River flood in 1887, and the Australian bush fires in 1983.
  ISBN 0-7894-2964-0
  1. Natural disasters —Juvenile literature. [1. Natural disasters.] I.
Title. II. Series.
GB5019.G75 1998
363.34'95—dc21   97-45222
                                                    CIP
                                                    AC
Color reproduction by Colourscan, Singapore
Printed and bound in Belgium by Proost

The publisher would like to thank the following for their kind
permission to reproduce their photographs:
t = top, b = bottom, l = left, r = right, c = center, m = middle

Andes Press Agency 38tl, 41tr (Caretas); Arquivo Fotografico 15t;
Barnaby's Picture Library/F Newman 45t; The Bridgeman Art
Library 14b; Andrew Burgess 7cl; Camera Press 4 l, 20b; Circus
World Museum 23b; Colorific!/Penny Tweedie 5bl, 43t; Corbis-
Bettman/Reuters 45b; Corbis-Bettmann/UPI 4 bl 22t 27t, 28, 29, 31t;
34t 35b, 36tl, 37tr, 41br; Mary Evans Picture Library 4cr, 9t, 15cl 16-
17b, 22b, 30tr, 31b, 33bl; Robert Harding Picture Library 4cl, 14t
(Guy Motil); Hulton Getty 33tr, 26t; Library of Congress 30-1b;
Ingrid Morejohn/Picture Works 18b, 20t; Pictor International 26b;
Planet Earth Pictures 4 br, 23tl, 24cl; Rex Features 19m; Science
Photo Library/ NASA 32 cl; South American Pictures/ Tony
Morrison 38cl; Frank Spooner Pictures 5cr (Brian Morrison), 46tr
(Bouvet/Hires/Duclos) 46b (Fornaciari-Nosca); Tony Stone Images
42bl (Ian Murphy), 42tr (Margaret Gowan); The Stock Market 4
bm, 40 (Ned Gillette), 5tr; Sygma 9b (De Gruey) 18t, 19t; Telegraph
Colour Library 33cr, 47br; Topham Picture Point 13, 23tl;
Wildlight/Philip Quirk 42tl; Woodfin Camp/Roger Werth 5cl, 8r.

Contents

Every year they kill, injure, or leave homeless millions of people.

Here are the stories of some of the worst natural disasters in history. The map below tells you where the disasters occurred, and where you can find them in this book. ❖

Hurricane winds
These winds can rip trees from the soil, toss cars around as if they are toys, and tear roofs off buildings.

Pompeii, Italy
(Volcano, AD 79)
Mount Vesuvius erupted, burying the Roman town of Pompeii under layers of ash and mud.
See pages 6–13.

ASIA

INDIAN OCEAN

AUSTRALIA

Yellow River, China
(Flood, 1887)
The Yellow River flooded China's Great Plain, killing two million people
See pages 18–21.

Southern Australia
(Bushfire, 1983)
A severe drought caused fires to rampage across the Australian bush.
See pages 42–45.

Lava flow
Red-hot lava may ooze gently from a volcano or be thrown high into the air by the force of the eruption.

Vesuvius
Farmers grew crops on Vesuvius. They had no reason to fear the volcano – it had been quiet for 800 years.

Take-out
At outdoor cafes, snacks were served from bowls sunk into the counter.

Vesuvius erupts!

ITALY, AD 79

It was a scorching-hot morning. At the foot of Mount Vesuvius, an inactive volcano in southern Italy, the Roman town of Pompeii baked in the August sunshine.

Despite the heat, Pompeii's streets and markets were bustling. The smell of fresh bread from bakers' ovens filled the air, and traveling musicians entertained the shoppers.

At a take-out restaurant, two women ordered snacks for their children. A man tied his dog to the counter and waited to be served.

In the packed taverns, people spoke excitedly about the afternoon's games in the amphitheater. This was a stadium where huge, bloodthirsty crowds gathered to watch trained warriors called gladiators fight each other – often to the death!

Just then, the ground trembled. The women at the take-out counter exchanged worried glances. Could it be another earthquake? They were common in the area but usually did little damage.

Suddenly there was a deafening boom – and the top of Mount Vesuvius blew right off!

Gladiator helmet
Gladiators were criminals or slaves. The most successful fighters were granted their freedom.

Amphitheater
Gladiator fights and chariot races were held in Pompeii's amphitheater.

Blast-off!
Hot, liquid rock moved up through the volcano until it blasted through the top of the mountain.

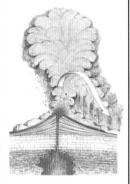

Unlucky wind
The force of the eruption broke the hot rock into billions of pieces of ash. Wind blew the deadly ash cloud toward Pompeii.

Mount Vesuvius was erupting! A fountain of fire shot upward and huge black clouds rose into the sky. The ground shook with the force of the explosion. People staggered, clinging tightly to one another.

The eruption of Vesuvius was similar to this 1980 eruption of Mount St. Helens in Washington State.

The women at the take-out restaurant pulled their children close. The dog barked wildly and strained at its lead. Taverns emptied and people ran from their homes, afraid to stay indoors in case the buildings collapsed.

Though it was daytime, darkness fell on Pompeii as ash and smoke blocked out the sun. Lightning bolts zigzagged through the towering cloud of ash above Vesuvius.

Smoldering ash and rocks – some the size of tennis balls – rained down from the sky. Crowds ran screaming through the gloomy streets, upsetting market stalls and trampling fruit and vegetables underfoot. Even gladiators training in the amphitheater dropped their weapons and ran.

Some people rushed to save precious objects. Others tied cushions or towels to their heads for protection as they fled the streets of Pompeii.

Eyewitness
A man named Pliny watched the eruption from a distance. This description is based on his eyewitness account of the disaster.

Raging sea
The water in the nearby Bay of Naples boiled as hot rocks and ash fell on its surface.

Hot ash stuck in people's throats. It got in their eyes and made them water. In no time at all, their clothes were coated in a layer of ash. As quickly as they brushed it off, a new layer formed!

Everyone was terrified. One man shouted, "The gods are angry with us! It's the end of the world!"

Another man prayed to the gods for help, wailing, "Have mercy on us!"

The ash piled up deeper and deeper. Soon it blocked the streets like a snowdrift. It filled rooms and caused roofs to cave in. The air became so thick with ash and choking fumes that it was impossible to breathe. The town was quickly disappearing under what looked like a blanket of gray snow.

About 2,000 people either chose to stay or were trapped in Pompeii. All of them died. Most of them suffocated or were crushed to death by falling buildings. But as many as 20,000 people managed to escape to the countryside.

In less than two days the town was buried under 15–20 feet (4.5–6 meters) of ash and rocks. Heavy rain set the ash hard like cement. The town of Pompeii then lay sealed in its rocky tomb for the next 1,800 years.

Roman gods
The Romans worshipped many gods and goddesses. Venus (above) was Pompeii's main goddess.

Volcanic ash
The eruption of Vesuvius threw ash so high into the air that it landed as far away as Africa and Syria!

Burned toast
Eighty-one loaves of bread, just ready to be eaten 2,000 years ago, were found in a baker's oven.

In 1860, the king of Italy ordered archeologists to uncover Pompeii. As they dug away the layers of rock, they were amazed to find the town almost exactly as it was when the volcano erupted – a pile of coins lay on the counter of a tavern, pots and pans stood on a hearth, a bowl of eggs had been placed on a table.

They also found that the bodies of the Pompeiians had rotted away and left hollow shapes in the rock.

This dog lays curled up in agony, still wearing his bronze collar and chain.

This cast shows a mother trying to shield her child from the ash.

The archeologists poured wet plaster into the hollows to make models of the bodies, called casts. When the plaster had set hard, the archeologists chipped away the surrounding rock and removed the casts. Many of them show people shielding their faces, clutching bags of jewels, or huddled together in terror.

The eruption of Vesuvius was a terrible event. But so many people and things were frozen in the moment of their destruction that today we have a priceless record of how the Romans lived at that time.

Mount Vesuvius is still an active volcano. It has erupted forty times since AD 79 – in 1631, 18,000 people died – and most recently in 1944. Who knows when it will decide to wake up again? ❖

Pompeii today
Today, it is possible to walk along the streets of ancient Pompeii.

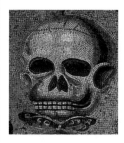

Scary reminder
This picture of a skull is from a house in Pompeii. It was meant to remind people that they should enjoy life while they could.

Lisbon
This is Lisbon today. In 1755 275,000 people lived in the city. It was the center of Portugal's empire, which stretched to South America.

Galleons
These huge ships brought precious cargoes such as gold, silver, silk, and spices from all over the empire.

Lisbon's great quake

PORTUGAL, SOUTHERN EUROPE, 1755

All was peaceful in Lisbon, the capital city of Portugal. Mighty ships called galleons were moored in Lisbon's harbor, their cargoes safely delivered. The streets were nearly empty. Most people were in church for the festival of All Saints Day, when worshippers remember loved ones who have died.

In the royal chapel, King José and his family bowed their heads in prayer. Candles burned steadily on the altar, and the smell of incense filled the air.

Suddenly there was a menacing rumble. Then another, lasting two full minutes, shook the city. It was the unmistakable shuddering of an earthquake! Church spires swayed like corn in a breeze. Inside the churches, bells clanged and chandeliers swung crazily.

Buildings tottered and then crashed to the ground, crushing the people inside.

A third tremor threw clouds of dust into the air, adding to the chaos and confusion. As the royal chapel began to crumble, the king and his family rushed outside. Hordes of people were running to the harbor to escape the falling buildings. But even there, they were soon to discover, they would not be safe.

King José I
José was king of Portugal between 1750 and 1777.

15

Giant waves
The giant waves that struck Lisbon's harbor were 50 feet (15 meters) high.

Destruction
Buildings that survived the quake were then gutted by flames.

When the crowds reached the harbor, they watched in horror as shock waves from the earthquake pulled the sea back for half a mile. Then the sea reared up and returned in three giant waves that smashed ships onto the shore and swept away the terrified onlookers.

Flames raced through the city as upturned candles set fire to wooden beams from collapsed buildings. Soon the city was a raging inferno. Lisbon was almost completely destroyed.

King José and his family escaped unharmed. But 60,000 people died and only 3,000 of the city's 20,000 houses were left standing.

Priests warned that an angry God had caused the earthquakes. But scientists suggested – for the first time in history – that earthquakes were the result of natural movements under the earth. ❖

River of Sorrow

Poor peasants
Peasants work on the land, growing crops and herding animals. They own land but are poor.

Yellow River
The river snakes through northern China to the Yellow Sea. Its name comes from the color of the clay it carries.

Life was tough for the Chinese peasant farmers who lived beside the mighty Yellow River. No matter how hard they worked each day in the fields below the river, they barely produced enough food to feed their families.

September 1887 saw a month of almost continuous rain. The river had begun to rise and people feared that it would burst its banks.

Over the centuries, the Yellow River had flooded the flat lands of China's Great Plain more than 1,500

times. The river had claimed so many lives and caused such tremendous suffering that it was known as "China's Sorrow."

Despite the threat of flooding, no one thought to leave. It was their home, and their families had lived there for hundreds of years. And it was harvest time – they would starve if they did not bring in their crops soon.

The rain continued to fall, and the river rose higher and higher. In some places it was already 15 feet (5 meters) above the surrounding flat lands. While some peasants gathered in the harvest, others set to work building embankments alongside the river. These embankments, called dykes, were their only hope of holding back the water.

But it was no use. At a sharp bend near the city of Zhengzhou, the fast-flowing river finally swelled over its banks. It tore a half-mile-long gap in the dykes, pouring a torrent of water onto the Great Plain.

Harvest crops
The peasants grew wheat, corn, rice, sweet potatoes, and a type of grass called sorghum.

Flood defense
For 2,500 years the Chinese have built dykes and dug channels to take the flood-water away.

Rafts
The peasants' straw and wicker rafts were similar to those used on the Yellow River today.

Disease
Drinking water that was contaminated by the flood led to disease.

Constant threat
The river has flooded often since 1887. In 1991, 1,270 drowned and 2 million were left homeless.

The flood swept away the peasants in the fields, but their cries were unheard above the noise of the rushing water. As the torrent reached the villages beyond the river, people climbed onto their roofs for safety. Some braved the flood in boats or rafts, rescuing people or throwing food to those marooned by the raging water.

The flood covered 11 cities and 1,500 villages, and killed 900,000 people. Thousands more died of disease and starvation. It took 18 months to fix the dykes and bring the river back under control.

Today, the flood defenses along the Yellow River are much improved. Dynamite has been used to alter the river's course to avoid dangerous bends, and plans have been made to build a huge, powerful dam. But the river will never be completely tamed. "China's Sorrow" will surely claim many more victims. ❖

21

Pelée awakes

Mount Pelée
This mountain was named after Pele, the Hawaiian goddess of volcanoes. A minor eruption 50 years before had covered the mountain with gray ash.

It was nearly 8:00 a.m., and the port of St. Pierre on the Caribbean island of Martinique was bustling. Sugar, rum, and bananas were being loaded onto ships, while rich French tourists strolled along the elegant streets. Local people toiled in the heat of the orchards and plantations.

Yet people were leaving town. Some were waiting for boats to take them off the island. Others were leaving by road. They were nervous because the usually quiet Pelée was belching smoke and ashes.

At night, red-hot cinders from Mount Pelée lit up the sky.

An official report had said there was no danger. But this did not stop the fear that gripped the town, and Governor Mouttet sent guards to keep more people from leaving.

Leon, the local shoemaker, watched the people leaving. He had lived here all his life and knew there was no cause for alarm.

In his jail cell, Auguste Ciparis wasn't concerned either. Locked away, without even a window, he knew nothing of events in the town.

23

Stopped watch
This watch melted to a stop at 8:15 a.m.

Bloodthirsty
The harbor at St. Pierre filled with hungry sharks attracted by the dead bodies floating in the water.

Suddenly Mount Pelée exploded with a sound like a thousand cannons firing. A glowing cloud of white-hot steam, dust, and gas rolled down the mountain – heading straight for St. Pierre!

The suffocating air killed most people instantly. Some tried to escape, but they were overtaken by the rapidly moving cloud. It was so hot that it burst open the skulls and stomachs of people as they fled.

Leon staggered into his house, clutching his chest. His lungs were racked with pain, and his skin was burning. He threw himself onto his bed, expecting to die. All around him things began to melt in the heat.

The streets ran with burning rum from flattened warehouses. Ships in the harbor capsized and sank as the fiery blast swept over them. In a matter of seconds, St. Pierre was reduced to a flaming ruin!

Glass wine bottle

Melting
Temperatures reached 1,800°F (1,000°C), melting objects like the wine bottle above.

Iron nails

Amazingly, Leon survived. But rescuers found no one else alive. Then, after four days, a faint cry was heard. Digging hard, they found Ciparis buried in the rubble of the prison. The thick walls of his cell had saved his life! He was later pardoned and granted his freedom.

The eruption of Pelée was the 20th century's worst volcanic disaster. Only two people survived. The rest of St. Pierre's 30,000 citizens were wiped out in a few minutes. ❖

Spoon and fork

San Francisco
The city began as a shanty town and grew rich from the gold rush of the mid 1800s.

Chinatown
Many Chinese laborers lived in Chinatown. They formed the largest Chinese community outside of the Far East.

Earthquake!
SAN FRANCISCO, CALIFORNIA, 1906

Dawn was breaking over the city of San Francisco. Two tourists named Carl and Pedro were strolling back to their hotel after enjoying the night-life in the city's Chinatown district.

The two friends were joking and chatting about the evening's fun. "What a night we've had!" said Pedro, laughing. Suddenly, Carl seemed to hurl himself against a wall. "Hey! Stop fooling around!" shouted Pedro. Then he, too, was thrown off-balance as the earth shook and heaved beneath his feet.

Bricks and broken glass showered down as buildings began to tilt and sway. "It's a quake, it's a quake!" cried a terrified man as he ran past.

Screams could be heard above the loud rumbling and grinding of the earthquake, as people fled their collapsing houses. Most were still dressed in their pajamas.

The tremors ended in a few minutes. Carl and Pedro looked around and saw that whole streets had been flattened by the earthquake. Even City Hall, which was supposed to be shockproof, had been shaken to pieces.

City Hall
The dome of the hall was left standing on a skeleton of girders.

27

Ham and Eggs Fire
One of the worst fires was the "Ham and Eggs Fire." It began when a woman cooked breakfast in her shattered home.

Fire trucks
The city's 38 horse-drawn fire trucks were no match for the 52 separate fires that broke out in San Francisco.

Earthquakes were nothing new to the people of San Francisco. The city sat on a great crack in the Earth's surface called the San Andreas Fault. Two chunks of the Earth's skin, called plates, meet at this fault. These plates slide against each other, sometimes causing earthquakes.

Carl and Pedro returned to their hotel but found only a heap of rubble. All the other guests had been crushed to death when it collapsed.

But the danger had just begun. Gas from broken pipes filled the air. Fires started as the flames from stoves and heaters, and sparks from severed electricity cables, ignited the gas. Soon whole streets were ablaze.

The water mains had shattered, too, so there was no water supply. Without water, the fire fighters had to battle the blazes with sewage. Restaurant owners broke open bottles of wine to dampen the flames.

Fire fighters blew up entire streets with dynamite, trying to create fire breaks – gaps between buildings to stop the flames from spreading. But the fires raged on.

Fire breaks
Most efforts to stop the fires by blowing up buildings simply created more fires.

The fires destroyed more buildings than the earthquake.

Looters
Thieves searched the rubble for valuables. Some were shot on sight by police.

Finally the fires died out. Only 500 people had been killed, but 200,000 people were left homeless. They slept on the streets or in Golden Gate Park, building shelters from whatever they could find. Some women gave birth to their babies on the grass in the park!

People searched the rubble for their belongings.

Rebuilding began immediately. Within four years, there was barely a trace of the quake's destruction.

Earthquakes still rock the city – a 1994 quake killed 61 people. But buildings are now constructed to withstand the tremors, and firefighting techniques have improved. San Francisco no longer has to be rebuilt after each earthquake. ❖

Makeshift stoves
People prepared their meals on temporary stoves until the electricity was restored.

Camps
Thousands of people lived in tents for up to three years after the earthquake.

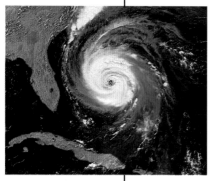

Long Island Express
NORTHEASTERN U.S., 1938

"Forecasters from the U.S. Weather Bureau are warning that a hurricane is heading toward Florida," said the report on the radio in Janice Kelly's Long Island home.

Janice heard the report, but her mind was on other things. Long Island, on the northeast coast of the U.S., was a long way from Florida. She was thinking about the rats that were scuttling around in her basement. Janice hated rats! She could not relax until her husband got rid of them.

Down in Florida, people started boarding up their houses. Hurricanes were a common occurrence. But as they worked, the hurricane changed direction. At first it seemed to be heading out to sea, where it would cause no harm. Then it turned north.

Gathering pace, it raced toward Long Island and the New England states like an express train. When it struck, it took everyone by surprise, toppling skyscrapers and demolishing homes as if they had been crushed by a giant steamroller!

Flying houses
In Madison, Connecticut, one house was lifted up and blown half a mile, and yet not a single window was broken!

Windy city
The force of the hurricane winds in New York was so strong that it caused the Empire State Building (above) to sway.

People fled from falling buildings, dodging the flying bricks.

The first place hit was Long Island. Families were relaxing on the beach, enjoying their picnics and watching their children build sand castles. Out at sea, the wind was whipping up huge waves. People who lived along the shore invited their friends to come and look at the big breakers.

Suddenly a wall of water 40 feet (12 meters) high rose up just off shore and crashed onto the beach, sweeping everyone away.

The sea surged inland, flooding towns along the coast. People were tossed about in the floodwaters. Some were rescued by those in higher buildings, who let down bedsheets and hauled them to safety.

Hurricane winds blasted across seven states, derailing trains and splitting roads. Floodwaters set off car horns. Their blaring added to the screams of the raging winds.

Toppled train
This train was surrounded by seawater and began to sink. Luckily, all the passengers escaped.

Flood damage
This road split into two when floodwater loosened soil underneath.

Wave power
In some places, the force of the waves changed the shape of the coastline permanently.

Destruction
The winds and the tidal wave they produced destroyed more than 57,000 houses. About 275 million trees were felled.

Janice Kelly and her husband clambered onto the roof of their house to escape the rising water. They were not the only ones to seek refuge on the roof. Three rats and a snake had beaten them to it! Janice shuddered. She hated rats! But the raging storm terrified her more.

Then, with a loud ripping sound, the wind tore the roof off the house! It swirled away across the bay, with the couple still clinging on. They closed their eyes, expecting to die.

Suddenly they jolted to a halt. They had come to rest on a golf course.

The Kellys looked across the bay to where their house once stood. Houses were flattened, cars were upturned and half-buried in mud, and nearly every tree had been uprooted. The roof had been a miraculous liferaft for the Kellys and their bedraggled animal passengers!

The hurricane devastated thousands of lives. Sixty thousand people were left homeless. The final death toll stood at more than 600. The "Long Island Express," as it was named, cut a path 325 miles (523km) long before it finally blew itself out. ❖

Paint stripper
The force of the wind scratched the paint off cars and stripped painted houses down to the bare wood.

Sea salt
Wind carried sea salt 120 miles (193 km) inland where it turned windows white.

Andes
This huge wall of mountains stretches along the entire Pacific coast of South America.

Peru's people
Peruvians are descendants of the ancient Inca people.

The highest
The Andes range is rising due to movements inside the earth. It may one day be the highest in the world.

Avalanche

PERU, SOUTH AMERICA, 1970

It was the end of May, and a group of Japanese friends were on a climbing vacation in Yungay. The town was a small but flourishing tourist resort that sat at the foot of towering Mount Huascaran in the Andes mountains of Peru. The locals, like most of soccer-mad Peru, were in the grip of World Cup fever. They had high hopes for the Peruvian team.

Each day the Japanese friends set off early to watch the sun rise over the Andes. At night, they sat under the 100-foot (30-m)- tall palm trees in the town square and listened to the excited chatter of the townsfolk.

One afternoon, while the friends were out climbing, a tremendous earthquake split apart the ocean bed just off the Peruvian coast. Earth tremors rippled right across mainland Peru.

It struck 23 minutes into the first World Cup game. Most of the locals were at home, following the match.

High up on Mount Huascaran, the Japanese climbers paused to enjoy the scenery. As they looked down at the quiet town, a low rumbling began. It seemed to grow louder and louder.

Then the mountainside far beneath them started to move. As they watched in horror, a huge mass of ice and rock cascaded down the face of the mountain. It was heading right toward the town!

Speed
An avalanche can move three times faster than highway traffic!

Boulders the size of houses hurtled down the mountain, part of a deadly wall of ice, mud, and rock. As the climbers watched, the wall hit the town and buried it.

The climbers hurried down to look for survivors, but Yungay had been wiped away. All that remained visible were the tops of four of the palm trees in the town square. The only survivors were a few people who had taken refuge in a hilltop cemetery at the edge of town.

Yungay was just one of many towns and villages devastated by the earthquake. The whole world was shocked by the scale of the disaster.

A short time later, Peru won its World Cup match against Bulgaria. The success helped lift the people's spirits as they began the long task of rebuilding their shattered lives. ❖

Rescue
It was three days before the mud was hard enough for rescuers to get to Yungay.

This statue of Jesus in the cemetery was the only thing not destroyed by the avalanche. 41

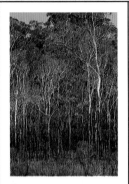

Bush
The bush is uncultivated land covered with scrub and trees.

Eucalyptus
These trees burn quickly because they have oil-filled leaves.

Bushfire

AUSTRALIA, 1983

It was the hottest February on record. In some parts of southern Australia it hadn't rained for four years. The wild country known as the bush was as dry as a bone. Koalas sheltered in eucalyptus trees, and kangaroos searched in vain for water.

On a farm near the city of Melbourne, Alan and Judy Watts looked at their scorched fields. "I'm worried," said Judy. "There've been fire warnings on the radio all day."

Out in the bush, the dry vegetation began to smolder and then catch fire in the sun's intense heat. Fanned by the wind, the small fires grew rapidly. Trees began bursting into flames. Fire fighters and groups of volunteers called "bush brigades" struggled hard to control the raging fire.

But soon a wall of fire 50 feet (15 meters) high was rolling over the land, reaching speeds of more than 70 miles (113 kilometers) per hour!

The Watts family saw the dark, dusty smoke heading toward them. In no time at all their home seemed to be surrounded by a towering wall of flames. Huge fire balls jumped across the farm road. There was no escape!

Bush brigades
These fire fighters carried water packs and spadelike beaters to put out the flames.

Ash clouds
In Melbourne, ash from the fire formed a thick crust over swimming pools.

"We've only got one chance – get in the water tank now!" shouted Judy. As the flames bore down upon them, they scrambled into the huge water-storage tank near the house. Standing in the water, they listened to the terrifying crackle of the fire as it stripped the forest of its trees. The raging fire made the water hotter and hotter, until it was almost unbearable. "We're going to be boiled alive!" thought Alan.

Finally the fire passed by, and the water began to cool. After ten hours, the Watts family hauled themselves out of the

tank. Dazed and exhausted, they peered through the smoky air. Their house was gone. Hundreds of farm animals lay dead on the blackened land. But they were alive.

At least 70 other people were not so lucky. A family of five died in their car as they tried to race away from the flames. Twelve fire fighters were engulfed in flames. The fire caused devastation. It destroyed seven towns and left 8,500 people homeless. The relentless flames also killed more than 200,000 cattle and sheep, and countless kangaroos and koalas. It is the worst bushfire in Australia's history. ❖

Charred earth
The fires left 150,000 acres (60,702 hectares) of land looking like a war zone.

Refugees
Temporary camps were built to house people left homeless by the fire.

This survivor was rescued after a volcanic eruption in Colombia, 1985.

Dealing with disasters

After a big disaster, rescue operations are often difficult and dangerous. Collapsed buildings crush many people to death but leave others trapped under the rubble. Flooded homes leave lots of people stranded. For rescuers, finding survivors is a race against time.

RESCUE EQUIPMENT

Trapped person detector

When thousands of people are buried alive, this machine finds survivors by detecting movement. This equipment helped save hundreds of lives after the Armenian earthquake in 1988.

Microphone enables rescuer to talk to trapped person

Thermal image camera

This camera is used after all kinds of disasters. It works by detecting the heat of a living person.

Sniffer dogs

Specially trained dogs help rescuers find survivors buried by mud or rubble.

Controls show if heat is present

Preparing for disasters

Living in disaster zones means monitoring volcanoes, fault lines, and weather patterns so that people can be prepared. Natural disasters cannot be prevented, but good planning can help reduce some of their worst effects.

Shake it up
Buildings in earthquake-prone regions are designed to withstand the deadly shaking. The Transamerica Pyramid in San Francisco looks fragile, but its cone shape makes it sturdier than a square-sided building.

Transamerica Pyramid

Everyday drills
In Japan and California, earthquake drills are part of everyday life. Children learn to keep a flashlight and sturdy shoes by their bed in case an earthquake strikes at night.

Snow stoppers
Forest trees planted above a village are the oldest and best way of slowing avalanches. Another device is a solid v-shaped stone wall, which can divide an avalanche so that it passes around a village or building. ❖

Glossary

Amphitheater
An open-air stadium.
The ancient Romans
watched gladiators fight
in the amphitheater.

Archeologist
An expert who digs up
ancient remains and tries
to work out what
happened in the past.

Avalanche
A huge fall of rock, ice,
and snow from the side
of a mountain.

Bush
An open, uncultivated
area of grasses, shrubs,
and trees.

Cast
A model made by pouring
plaster or molten metal
into a hollow mold.

Crust
The earth's outer layer,
made up of huge slabs of
rock that rest on a bed
of liquid rock.

Drought
A long period with very
little rain or no rain at all.

Dyke
A wall built alongside a
river or canal to hold
back floodwater.

Earthquake
A shaking of the ground
caused by movement of
the segments that make
up the topmost layer of
the earth.

Eruption
The explosion of a
volcano, which may
throw out lava, steam,
ash, dust, suffocating
fumes, and hot gas.

Fire break
A gap that is made by
fire fighters in a forest or
between buildings to stop
a fire from spreading.

Forecaster
A scientist who studies
the weather and predicts
how it will change.

Galleon
A large sailing ship with
three or four masts.
Galleons were used from
the 15th to the 18th
centuries as warships and
trading vessels.

Gladiator
A trained fighter in the
ancient Roman empire,
who battled against
other gladiators or wild
animals for the
entertainment of the
Roman citizens.

Governor
A person who rules, or
governs, a place.

Hurricane
A terrible storm with a
swirling mass of powerful
winds at its center.

Incense
Special sticks that are
burned for their fragrant
fumes.

Lava
Red-hot liquid rock from
inside the earth that
bursts on to the surface.

Looters
People who steal things
from a disaster scene.

Monsoon
The rainy season in
tropical regions.

Natural disaster
A destructive event
caused by the forces
of nature.

Plain
A large expanse of level
land in the open country.

Plates
Segments of the earth's
crust. These large slabs
of rock cover the earth's
surface like a giant
jigsaw puzzle.

Skyscraper
A tall building consisting
of many stories, usually
built of concrete and steel.

Tremor
A trembling of the
ground. Earthquakes are
usually made up of a
number of powerful
tremors, coming one
after the other.

Volcano
A mountain with a
central crater through
which hot gases, ash, and
molten rock sometimes
burst out.